Beyond Language

Beyond Language

A Philosophical Journey

VERN R. WALKER

RESOURCE *Publications* • Eugene, Oregon

BEYOND LANGUAGE
A Philosophical Journey

Resource Publications
An Imprint of Wipf and Stock Publishers
199 W. 8th Ave., Suite 3
Eugene, OR 97401

www.wipfandstock.com

PAPERBACK ISBN: 978-1-6667-0153-1
HARDCOVER ISBN: 978-1-6667-0154-8
EBOOK ISBN: 978-1-6667-0155-5

07/06/21

For Elizabeth,
giver of meaning

Contents

Preface

YOU AND I ARE minor moments within a flowing river of language. What lies beyond our bubbles, and beyond the river's banks, is the subject of this book. River creatures, we cannot see or touch what lies beyond, but we guess its existence. For we experience the force and ebbs of water flow, and we can surmise the nature of language. Language makes us what we are, and it determines who we can be.

This book has been in the writing for many years, centuries, and millennia. It has come to flow through me from a long line of philosophers—Heraclitus and Parmenides, Plato and Aristotle, Hume and Kant, Hegel and Husserl, Whitehead and Wittgenstein, Kierkegaard and Sartre and Camus. The words have come together through the fighting in central Vietnam, through practicing law in Washington, and through teaching both philosophy and law. Like all currents within language, its course has been shaped by history, by circumstances, by a thousand personal choices, and by the hidden laws that govern word flow.

The book took its present shape amid the red rock formations of Sedona, Arizona. But as prehistoric and post-historic as those vistas are, more magnificent still is the spring flood of language that creates you and me. Even more profound is our mysterious pursuit of what and who we are. This is a book about that spring flood and mysterious pursuit, and about realizing our roles in the universe beyond language.

PART I

Describing the Present Moment

NAMING IS A GAME we learned very young, as naturally as catching a ball. Large, soft balls and simple words at first, until we learned to catch them and toss them back. I watch in wonder as young children begin to play catch with words. They begin to see the world not only with their eyes but also with their words. We give them our world when we teach them our words.

A system of names is like a system of road signs, telling us what lies down this road or down that road, how to reach this or that destination, which places can be reached by this highway exit or by the next one. Words name things the way road signs provide directions. Names are simply signs, although there is nothing simple about signs. To understand language, we need to understand signs, or what it is that makes a sign a sign. We begin our journeys in life by learning how to describe the present moment.

1

Sensations

I DO NOT REMEMBER learning to catch a ball or learning my first words. At the earliest time I can remember, I already knew how to play catch and how to speak. This is an essential clue. I have now taught my own children their first words, just as my parents undoubtedly taught me. Playing catch with words: "What color is this?" "Blue." Simple names of colors and textures and tastes; names for balls and foods and people. I taught my children the same durable names that I have used all my life.

I seem to have names for very few of the colors I can see. Perhaps several dozen names, such as "red," "blue," and "black." "Light red" and "pink," "dark blue" and "gray." I can see, however, thousands of different colors. The wide array of greens I see in a forest as the light changes; the uncounted shades of red in a brilliant sunset. Few of these colors have names. I can make do with variations on the words "green" and "red."

The other senses fare even worse in naming. For the sense of touch, there are sensations of "smooth" and "rough," "hard" and "soft," "cold" and "hot." Degrees of these have a few more names, such as "little" and "very," "less" and "more." We also use similarity or source to make names: "smooth as silk," "hard as nails," "cold as ice." But many perceptible touches have no names at all.

For sounds, we sometimes imitate the sound itself. "Click," "chuckle," or "blast"; "whoosh," "whine," or "roar." The imitation *is* its name. We can adjust the volume by talking loudly or softly, or by saying "loud" or "soft." We also name sounds by naming the things that make them—the sound of a waterfall, or the sound of thunder, or a police siren. But at a music concert or in a schoolyard of children, I hear many sounds that have no names.

Tastes and smells are impoverished for names. Beyond a few words like "sweet" or "salty" and their opposites, we name the things that produce the tastes—oregano and ginger, pepper and mint. The taste of my simmering sauce, however, has no name except "the taste of the sauce." Similarly with smells—of smoke or roses or garlic. The smell of garlic from the kitchen may be "strong" or "faint," but the aroma from the sauce is merely "delicious."

Poets and merchants push back against the poverty of language for sensations, inventing new expressions. But the inevitable poverty tells us much about language.

Cool breezes play
Across my face—
Chilling the tear
Teased from my eye
And rubbing more moisture
From my dry skin.
To the wind,
I am part of the hard red rock
On which I sit.
I watch the white desert sun
Flare silently
As it rises
Above the ridge line—
Glaring at me,
Blinding me for staring at it.
I close my eyes
In submission,
The world suddenly reduced
To the thick red glow
Of eyelids
Cooled by wind.

Part I: Describing the Present Moment

Naming is a game created and played by family and community. We teach our children to play catch with balls and words, just as we were taught. Throw a question; throw back a word in answer.

While catching balls and naming colors, we also learned success and failure. We somehow learned that the goal was to keep the ball from falling to the ground and to pick the right name for the color. There is a right and wrong use of color words. Naming does not belong to you and me, to do with entirely as we wish. A mistaken word can cause confusion or misunderstanding; a defiant misuse of words can bring punishment for lying. We usually enjoy playing the game well—we love to talk, to be understood, to be taken seriously. You know what I mean when I use words, most of the time.

If we want more names there are ways to invent them to suit our purposes—for choosing paint ("metallic avocado mist"), playing music ("three-quarter time"), selecting wines ("dry, full-bodied"). We can name whatever we find of interest, or have need to name.

But most of my many sensations have no names, and are noticed necessarily in silence. Are such sensations beyond language? We would not say so. Even the shade of red between the two shades that I can name has a name: it is at least "a shade of red between those two shades of red." If I see a distinct color, can I not name it if I want to? Is there a difference between being aware of something and being able to name it? Are my sensations merely events in river flow, or are there connections with dry earth? If I throw you questions such as these, are there answers that we call "correct"?

2

Emotions and Moods

A TODDLER'S WORLD IS filled with more than colors and tastes and sounds. It also contains pain. We teach our children words like "hurt" when they cut their fingers, and "burn" when they touch a hot pan. We use such words as though they are names—names for "feelings." Some feelings are so localized to touch and so familiar, that giving them names seems to work well enough. Those feelings are somehow close enough to being in the public world. They are "in" our fingers.

As my children grow older, I begin to talk to them about their "emotions" and "moods." A few emotions, such as anger or happiness, fear or excitement, are so common and so tied to circumstance and behavior that I do not hesitate to name them. The tantrum and the laughter are symptoms for diagnosis, much like fever and chills are for illness. The emotion, like the disease, we talk of being "deeper inside," but detectable from "outside."

More difficult still are moods like anxiety and hope, pride and shame and resentment. Which of these is my child experiencing at any moment? It is sometimes hard to say. I have enough difficulty naming them correctly in myself. I am unsure what my feelings are—that is, which names to give them. And yet being correct can be important. "Fear" of what? "Anxiety" when? "Guilt" due to what? Playing catch with such words is unsettling, not knowing whether we have dropped the ball.

Moods often seem to blend many emotions at once, much like the complex blending of sensations when hearing music played or experiencing a thunderstorm. Envy and fear, frustration and inadequacy, seem to be close cousins. It is difficult to say which moods I have, or how many, or when they begin and end.

Perhaps lovers dare the most in trying to name emotions and moods. I want to tell you what I feel, but how will you interpret my words? I want to know what you feel without being told, but how will I know if I am wrong? In this important game of catch, our abilities seem least when needs are greatest.

We risk much in naming. Words create moods as well as name them, making us happy, or angry, or anxious. Emotions and moods blur the lines between recognition and creation, between naming and expressing. We would like to think, I suppose, that when we care about each other, those lines no longer matter. And yet they seem to matter more.

She looked up at me
Surprised,
Her hurt holding
My eyes hostage—
Waiting for me to speak.
The blood suddenly vanished
From my head,
And my heart jumped
To replace it,
As words choked my throat, and
Remorse spread sour
Upon my tongue.
With hot shame shooting
Up my face,
I stammered,
"I'm sorry.
I didn't mean it."
In slow, silent sorrow
She read my face—
Dropped her eyes—
Nodded slightly.
Nothing more to say.

Part I: Describing the Present Moment

Our everyday thinking tells us that we can name sensations of color correctly because we all see the same objects and share a common biology of vision. These facts seem to explain our remarkable success in creating names for such sensations and correcting mistakes when they are made. But the community is less able, or less willing, to police the use of words that refer to emotions and moods. Unlike naming colors, I cannot point out my emotions to you; unlike tasting pieces of fruit, I cannot hand my emotions to you to sample. Beyond cut-finger pain and joyful laughter, the practice of "naming correctly" runs into difficulty.

Naming correctly is a game that works only in community. To name the color of the ball *correctly* is to give it the name that others would give it. We want to say that naming my present mood correctly is to call it what you and others would call it if the mood were yours. But is consensus everything? Is describing my mood correctly nothing more than our agreeing on a word to use? Did my parents determine what I'm feeling when they taught me how to speak?

Is introspection easier or harder than naming sensations and feelings in other people? As teenagers we wondered whether you and I were experiencing the "same" mood, feeling the "same" emotion. How would we ever know? It was a good question then, and remains a good question now, even though we adults no longer try to answer it. We say we live with "private inner worlds," where most feelings flow unnamed. Getting along with each other in one "public outer world" seems somehow more important. But why do we pretend that naming correctly is still the game we are playing?

3

Thoughts

MY SENSATIONS, EMOTIONS, AND moods come bundled together. Smooth red balls bounce and make me laugh, hot food tastes delicious and satisfies my hunger, lightning and thunder shake the house and terrify me. In my experience, outer and inner flows run together.

By giving names to selected bundles, we identify individual things—"smooth red bouncy ball"; "hot salty vegetable soup"; "frightened little boy." By the time I was old enough to think about it, the habit of bundling words to name things had become a foundation for my consciousness. Sharing lists of names about familiar objects was how you and I spent much of our time together growing up.

I have taught my children the same tricks we were all taught—to bundle some things "inside" of us, others "outside." The "sharp pain" is in my cut finger, but not in the knife. The "feeling of happiness" is inside me, not in the rose. You and I can be in the same room, looking at the same object, but you feel embarrassment while I think the situation is rather funny. There is an "outside" world of objects that is distinct from my "inside" world.

The outside world is "objective" because the community enforces correct naming for it. Everyday thinking bundles qualities of physical objects "outside," like "hard balls" and "red bicycles." The world of "objectivity" is the world of correct naming, of the "true" and the "false."

Part I: Describing the Present Moment

By contrast, sensations and feelings we bundle together "inside," in private realms "within" each of us. Yet sensations are closely tied to the objective world. The color of the bicycle may be outside, and my sensation of that color is inside, but I can name both incorrectly. Deeper inside my subjective world, I have more freedom to name my emotions and moods.

I am the center of an outside world connected to an inside world. "Outside" things I experience through sensation and emotion. Some taste sweet to me and others bitter, the wind chills me as rain drenches my clothing. "Inside," I enjoy your company, I am lonely when you have gone, I hope to see you again soon. My body has sensations, feelings, and thoughts inside.

You are also the center of an outside world connected to your inside world. So are billions of other people. Our talk about "outside" and "inside" makes it possible for billions of people and worlds to exist at the same time.

Thoughts

I had forgotten
How long a drive it is
To my parents' house.
With the vibrations of road and engine
Still humming in my back and legs,
I walk stiffly toward the front door,
My muscles objecting to movement
But yearning for more.
The brass knob of
Cold smooth metal
Turns in my hand,
The heavy wooden door
Gives way reluctantly—
Releasing in a rush
The moist heat,
Kitchen smells, and
Small shrieks of laughter—
New life exploding out of a small space,
Pushing excitedly into the future,
Yet echoing voices from years ago.
My brother and his children
Have arrived home before me.

Connection is the essence of thought—not just names, but names connected. Thinking connects names to names, creating things. We are makers of bundles, and we are bundles of things; connectors of things and connected to them.

We say that your pain, excitement, and sadness are "inside" you because we cannot see them the way we see your dark hair and brown eyes. But they are not "inside" you like an object is "inside" a room. *"Inside of you,"* in that sense, are only muscles, heart, and brain. Curiously, the word "in" seems to name many different ways of connecting things—the ball is "in" the room, the pain is "in" my finger, and the thought is "in" my head. But pains and thoughts are not objects at all, and the word "in" is not the name of any thing. Thoughts are streams of words running through my head. But "run" here doesn't mean *run* and "through" doesn't mean *through*. Thoughts do not run through my head like the blood runs through it.

A moment ago, when you read the sentence "Thoughts are streams of words running through my head," you knew what I meant. When you read that sentence, did thoughts run through your head as a stream of words? What were they doing, those words? Perhaps a few seemed to name, such as "head." Perhaps others, such as "are" and "through," were not naming at all, but just connecting names to names, or words to other words. Although naming began as playing catch with words, words later began to play games of tag among themselves. And we began to play other games with words.

PART II

Space and Time

LANGUAGE HOLDS OUR EXPERIENCES together in space and time. Every object is connected to every other objective thing in space and time. Every event in time is connected to every other event. Sensations, feelings, and thoughts are events connected to each other in time, and if we locate them "inside" our bodies, then they are connected to objective things in space as well. Language connects every thing together: words to things, words to words, and things to things.

Language is like a highway system that we use to travel at high speeds from one place to another. Using words to name or refer to things is like getting on or off the highway system. Words mark locations in the system, and "having a thought" is arriving at such a location. To think is to travel along the highway; to speak is to take our hearers along a route; to listen is to be taken along it. This book is taking you on a particular tour of the language countryside.

The highway system constrains where we can go with speed. Most people are busy getting on with life—using roads, not building them. Few try to travel the mountainous terrain on foot.

Between us, we map the space and time around us. Questions are uttered strings of words requesting directions, and answers are uttered strings of words telling the way. Question-and-answer is a highly durable game we learned to play as children, and the wise play it all their lives.

4

Space

QUESTIONS ABOUT "WHO" AND "what" are inquiries about names. "Who is that?" I ask, and you answer "John." "What is that?" you ask, and I answer "ball." Two kinds of name? "The boy with the ball is named John."

Questions about "where" or "how far" ask about names of locations and spaces. I taught my children the meaning of "Where is the ball?" by supplying answers like "in the house." I accepted only certain kinds of answers as sensible. If I thought their responses were not correct answers, I corrected them, as though my children were misunderstanding me, or joking, or playing some other game. By connecting sensible answers with their own perceptions and actions, my children learned the meaning of "across the yard," "down the street," "near the stream."

Names for spatial relationships can make actions more effective. A community can find food or avoid danger through coordinated use of words like "here" and "there," "turn right" or "turn left," "far ahead" instead of "close behind." Commerce, navigation, and construction depend on *correctly* naming shapes, such as "rectangle" and "circle" and "sphere." Location and spatial relationships are so important that we have invented words to name every possible configuration.

And we invent more serious games. Claims of perception might assert spatial relationships among physical objects: "seeing" a ball over there, "tasting" this soup, "hearing" the distant thunder.

But such claims are also assertions about truth. If I claim to *see* a red ball over there, then I am claiming to be in a position to see that there actually is a ball over there that is red. I normally expect you to be able to see it also. If it *appears* to me that there is a red ball, then I am entitled to claim that I *see* a red ball, at least under normal viewing conditions. This is the way our language of perception works.

A claim of success is of course no guarantee of success. I may claim to see a red ball, but I could be mistaken—it may not be a ball, or it may not be red. A claim of perception, like any claim of truth or falsehood, may seem to be warranted when it is not. Saying or thinking that I caught the ball is not the same as catching it. Saying or thinking or claiming that I saw a ball does not mean I actually saw one.

Space

The red rock mesa
Is many miles further
Than it looks—
I could die
Well before getting there
In this heat.
The pale mountain ridge
Is probably many miles more,
Beyond the mesa—
More than a lifetime of steps
From here.
I sit wearily
Upon the trail,
A long way
From where I need to be.
The small stones at my feet
Ignore me
With profound indifference—
Cousins to the mesa
And the mountain,
They do not care
What happens next.

Part II: Space and Time

Our survival depends on successful naming of measurements. The true name of that distance may be "twelve miles," and the actual amount of water in my bottle may be "seven ounces." Lives depend on surviving desert journeys, constructing sturdy shelters, subdividing farmland fairly, building safe roads and the vehicles to use on them. Error, like illusion and hallucination, can be dangerous.

Miraculously, all the physical objects existing at the moment seem to fit precisely into space. All accurate measurements are perfectly consistent with each other. Any inconsistent measurements can be resolved. But why do objects fit together in space in such an orderly way? Is this an extraordinary coincidence of nature or an extraordinary accomplishment of thought and language?

One way we keep space unified and consistent is by removing from it our sensations of color, sound, and taste, our feelings and our emotions, and our thoughts. In that way, we do not have to reconcile in space the blue surface that I see with the green surface that you see, what tastes sweet to me with what tastes bitter to you. We unify space in part by saying that sensations, feelings, and thoughts are "inside" of us—by which we mean that they do not take up space. But can the trick be that easy? Can we subtract anything from the outside world if it causes trouble with our spatial game of catch? What remains "objective" and "outside" if sensations of color and sound become "subjective" and "inside"? What are objects really like, if not how they look or taste? And where are they when they are in the past?

5

The Past

SOMEHOW, WE EXPERIENCE CHANGE. Plants flower and produce fruit, warm days turn cold, discordant sounds give way to melodies. The mountains do not seem to change location, but they do seem to change color as I watch shadows move across them. Physical objects exist "through time," we say, and changes are events that happen to objects.

"Where do objects go when they no longer exist?" seems a nonsense question to adults, who have become accustomed to our games about time. There is no sense to the question—it is not a game we play. We do say that they are "in the past," but the past is not a place or a spatial container for objects to be "in."

We invent new meanings and new names for time relationships. "In the evening, after we had eaten dinner, we walked down to the shore just before the sun set." This morning and yesterday, weeks and months and years—we measure the past differently than we measure space, and relate events differently than we relate locations.

Yet we say we (accurately) "remember" the past much like we (accurately) "perceive" the present. We compare memories, try to reconcile inconsistent versions, and develop methods for deciding accuracy. We encourage success at remembering, and consider failure to be a sign of problems. Our common story is that our sensations and emotions of the present leave memory traces inside of us after they are past. My memories are present echoes of my past experiences.

Remembering that it rained yesterday is not like remembering that Rome once ruled an empire, although I am entitled to claim to remember both. But I saw it rain yesterday, while I have only listened to teachers or read books about Rome. Even traveling to see Roman ruins establishes little, unless I am correctly told that what I am seeing are ruins that date from Roman times, and not fabrications from the recent past. The stories that historians tell us give as much significance to the stones as the stones give to the stories. Stories hold my sensations and memories together and turn them into one connected whole about the past-and-present.

The sun settles slowly
On the mountain rim,
Then silently slides
Behind it—
The lingering reds
And deepening blues
Becoming black.
For me
These are the colors of sadness
When she is not here,
Her hand warm in mine
And her shoulder soft
Against me.
How many sunsets
Have we shared,
She and I—
Seen over sharp-edged oceans
Or through tree tops at meadow's edge,
In rain-departed mists
Or soft clear air?
Some would count the years,
But I prefer to count
The sunsets.

Remembering the past is no less mysterious than perceiving the present. Then and now, there and here, outside and inside, object and sensation—all are learned and not learned, a fusion of language and reality. The "subjective" and "cultural" penetrate the "objective" in deep and stubborn ways. Just like I had to learn what it means to say "I am seeing a red ball in the distance," I had to learn what it means to say "I remember that a red ball was in my room yesterday." Just like I had to learn what it means to say "Rome once ruled an empire." Is there anything *not* learned in any of this?

Need all past events fit precisely into time, the way that all present objects fit into space? What does it matter? What difference would it make? You and I might describe differently the "same" event, but this is also true of objects. We can tolerate imprecision with many past events, but when we bring a table home we want it to fit in the space we remember measuring for it.

"How do we know we are all remembering the ball correctly?" is a meaningful question deserving an answer. It is a game we collectively choose to play. "How do we know the world didn't begin yesterday, with all our memories created in it?" is not a serious question for most of us, even if it looks like one, and a few people might treat it as worthy of an answer. Some questions cast doubt on the very activity of remembering anything at all. This is not a game the community wants to play. What would be the point of playing such a game? Without remembering there would be no past; without a past there would be no change; and without change there would be no conscious life at all. Denying memory would be a kind of suicide.

6

The Future

THE FUTURE IS VERY different from the past, although neither exists in the present and both provide endpoints for change. The past is nothing any more; the future is nothing yet. The difference is that I *perceive* objects in the present and I *remember* events in the past, but I seem to have no similar awareness of the future. I have been taught that I must wait until events occur before I can experience them. I can only experience events in the present, as they go sliding into the past. Our games about how we relate to the future are not the same as how we relate to the present or the past.

We generally agree that events in the past are fixed and can never be changed, but we debate whether events in the future are determined by those in the past. Some say that future events are just as fixed as past events, only they are as yet unknown to us. But this view of fate does not confine our language. We talk about what "might happen if," what "could occur," and what "is possible." The question of fate goes deeper than whether you and I have free will— it is a puzzle about the nature of the future itself.

Future events are not entirely formless. The language we have developed about the present and past structures our thoughts about the future. Possible future events become the present if they actually happen. Then the objects in those events fit into space, and those events interlock with events in the past. We ask-and-answer many meaningful questions about the future, using the same descriptive language that we use about the present and past. We may be uncertain about what will occur, but it is uncertainty within the scope of possibilities.

I have wondered sometimes whether I can "see into" the future, but I have been convinced it is only "imagining." And what I imagine may or may not be real. Imagining is merely imaging "inside my mind." I might imagine a scene over the horizon, or imagine a past event as though I had been there. So too I can imagine what a future scene might look like. But imagining does not make it so, we say.

Some people seem more successful than others at predicting what the future will bring, at least on average. Our friends predict what we will like or dislike. Our experts advise us on weather and sports and even economic conditions. But where would friends or experts get such knowledge?

Goodbyes always
Look forward,
Being made at the edge
Of whatever is to come.
Some farewells are sought—
The necessary preludes
To adventure;
Others arrive unbidden
And unwanted,
Pushing us
Into the future
Against our wills.
Goodbyes are the bittersweet
Edges of the now—
First days of school,
Graduations,
Lovers parting in airports.
No one is ever left behind—
We all go forward
From our goodbyes—
Only not together.

Part II: Space and Time

We are convinced that tomorrow will come, although we are not sure what it will bring. Physical objects and space seem so durable, that we learn to count on their being there in the future. Particular objects may "go out of existence"—rocks are crushed, bridges collapse, people die and their bodies decay—but other objects take their places. In any event, space itself remains intact, even where empty.

I *might* wake up tomorrow and see an ocean where today I see ancient mountain peaks. I can imagine it. But I do not wager that the mountains will be gone. Such a thing hasn't happened yet, as far as we can tell. Are future possibilities as real as the present or the past, or are they not real at all? What would the word "real" mean here? Why would we use such words in such a way?

If the sun itself burns out in the future and the word "tomorrow" loses its natural meaning, we think that there would still be time after that. Time, we say, is "eternal" and "without end." We talk that way without hesitation, without puzzlement—and without any evidence. It is simply part of everyday thinking. But why would we tell ourselves such a story? And what can such a story mean?

PART III

Everyday Thinking and Science

THE FUTURE CREATES THE possibility of error, as our memories of the past insistently remind us. Thinking that the surface of the stove is cold, I touch it, burn my finger, and realize that my belief (now past) was false. Life itself often depends on accurate prediction, so ways of talking and thinking evolve that improve our chances of success—at least for some of us, in some circumstances, on average. These ways of talking range from everyday thinking to careful science.

We build language for the same reason that we build roads—to connect places where people want to go. The road system is continuously under construction, in dynamic adjustment to the plans and desires of communities. So too with language.

The grammar and meaning of language provide the basic structure of the system, including both its layout and its traffic laws. Grammar and meaning determine where we are able to go in the system. Without grammar and meaning to provide structure among words, traveling would be only random and solitary wandering.

Using words grammatically and sensibly, we evolve our everyday thinking. Science invents new language on top of this everyday thinking, to extend and refine our abilities in certain directions, for certain purposes.

But the structure of language and the structure of the world need have little in common. Language is not a picture of the world. Language exists to get the traveler to a destination, and it need not mirror the world to do that.

7

Measuring

THE TWO BASIC PRACTICES of everyday thinking and science are classifying things and then counting the things that we have classified. There is no new mystery here. Classifying is naming. Naming an object or event assigns a word to it; classifying creates groups by assigning the same word to numerous things. The child who learns what "red ball" means is learning how to use correctly the words "red" and "ball." The child also learns that the practice of naming can classify many things into the same group. To invent a common name or description is to create a new possible group. Mathematicians call such groups "sets."

Closely related to this activity of classifying is the practice of "counting" the things we have classified. Counting is a rigorous method of naming. The question, "How many balls are there?" is a request to name their count. I trained my children how to perform a count correctly, as well as the correct words to use when counting, such as "one" and "two" and "seven." We also use such words to name sets of things by size, counting the things grouped into them. There are "seven balls" in the box.

The measuring methods of science use the classifying and counting practices of everyday thinking, only refined and extended and rigorously enforced. From counting objects jumbled in a box, we arrange them end-to-end in space, and develop our practice-concepts of measurement for distance, area, and volume, as well as the other practice-concepts of geometry. We also extend our classify-and-count activities to time—dividing days into hours, twilights into minutes, the immediate past into seconds. We extend these practice-concepts for quantifying time to the future as well as to the past. By inventing such measurement methods and language, everyday thinking and science have transformed the space and time of individual experience into a single continuum.

As soon as children learn words for sensations, thoughts, and things, they have acquired a communal framework of space and time. This world of everyday experience is the same world measured by science.

Measuring

The airplane pushed itself
Off the runway
With an effort,
The engine whine working its magic.
Perhaps I will not die this time either.
I recite safety statistics
To my anxious stomach,
And divert my attention
To the human creation
Spreading out beneath the window—
Tall buildings and street mazes,
Suspension bridges and power lines,
Geometric fields of greens and browns.
Finally the plane's engines
Begin to calm themselves,
Reassured by
Readings on cockpit instruments,
Entries in maintenance logs,
Test results on metal fatigue.
We thrust ourselves high
Into the future,
Supported only by air
And numbers.

Technology is everyday thinking and science applied to human action. When irrigating farms or designing engines, running businesses or constructing bridges, we seem to do better when we take careful measurements of all the things that matter. Amounts of rainfall and evaporation volumes, heat transfer rates and friction coefficients, prices of raw materials and demand schedules, hardness of metals and burn-times of fuses. The practice of measurement is validated by success.

Technological success seems to prove the objectivity of measurement. Acts of classifying-and-counting that lead to more successful outcomes prove that we are accurately measuring the real object, not merely naming your or my sensations. Everyday thinking and science have so far succeeded well by dividing the "outside" world from "inside" minds, the "objective" from the "subjective"—and then by measuring the "objective outside" and discounting the "subjective inside."

Science confirms that everyday physical objects exist and that the space and time in which they exist are real. It is a fact that two plus two equals four, and never equals five or red. Our success when using geometry, mathematics, and scientific measurement convinces us that these activities measure objects as they really are.

What am I to think, however, when physicists tell us that everyday objects consist almost entirely of empty space, and that all the mass in the universe was compressed, billions of years ago, into a space smaller than the tip of my finger? Should I choose the language of everyday thinking or the language of science, or should I just ignore the apparent contradiction?

8

Predicting

MEASUREMENTS OF THE PRESENT sometimes allow accurate predictions about the future. We use barometers to predict stormy weather, color and texture to predict crop spoilage, bodily symptoms to predict the course of illness. Our survival strategy is to classify things in useful ways, take accurate measurements of them, make predictions based on those measurements, and then take timely action. The possibility of accurate prediction makes planning both useful and prudent. Error can be deadly.

Predicting is a complicated enterprise, however, with many things that can go wrong. If observations are sloppy, or measurements are faulty, or inferences incorrect, then actions can be ineffective or even harmful.

Common sense has a storehouse of advice for action and prediction, reflecting the remembered experiences of the community. Advice about how to obtain food to prevent starvation, how to cook meats to avoid illness, how to deal with people who might not be trustworthy. Adages like "look before you leap" are learned from generation to generation.

Science invents new ways of identifying, classifying, and connecting events that occur with regularity. Whenever possible, scientists conduct experiments in which they carefully measure every circumstance—the conditions under which they conduct the experiment, the objects that are involved, and all the relevant events that occur. Experimenting is a systematic search for connections that might prove useful in making predictions.

Because life is deadly and the future uncertain, because we desire good things and strive to attain them, many of our thoughts and discussions, concepts and practices, are devoted to predicting the future and recording stories of success and failure from the past. Common sense tells us to be practical and anticipate the future. Science shows us methods of making more accurate and precise predictions. Knowledge is therefore power in the combination of everyday thinking, science, and technology. We have no choice about whether to go into the future, but perhaps we have some small influence on where and how to enter it.

Will I succeed
Or will I fail?
What will become of me?
History is peopled by failures—
Insurrections crushed,
Cities drowned in volcanic ash,
Wealth squandered or stolen.
For every storied success there are
A thousand forgotten failures.
There are so many ways
To go wrong,
And so few right—
So many people
Pushing to succeed,
When so few can.
Common sense gives me
The same advice that it gives you—
Study success,
Strengthen skills,
Aim for what you love,
But learn to love
The best that you can do.

When predictive error can be costly, we spend a great deal of time arguing about it. And everyday thinking and science are often at odds. At one time in the past it was everyday thinking that the sky is a dome, the earth is flat, or the sun travels daily around the earth. We now have good evidence that ships never reach the edge of the earth, that earth and sun both hurtle through space, and that the universe is vast. Science has changed the everyday thinking of many people on those ideas.

But today there are new anxieties over nuclear energy and genetic engineering. Common sense warns against allowing people to experiment with catastrophe. Technology is not just science applied to everyday thinking, but power in the hands of certain people. Scientific language is the technology of the true, and power in the hands of scientists, and of those who pay for science. But what will they do with this technology, these newly powerful people? It is hard to predict.

In predicting human behavior, scientists have rather minimal success. Psychologists keep inventing categories for classifying people and behaviors—personalities and their disorders, abilities and disabilities, values and prejudices. Sociologists and economists invent more categories—family types and cultures, organizations and movements, political systems and economic structures. With new categories come new measurements and more data. Yet despite the abundant data, we are making too little progress when it comes to predicting people. Is it prudent to empower without being able to predict its use?

9

Explaining

THE GREATEST ACHIEVEMENTS OF both everyday thinking and science are not the data gathered or the facts established, not the space-and-time connections discovered or the theories so far proven. The greatest inventions are the two practice-concepts of "proving" statements to be true or false, and "explaining why" they are true or false. From these two related activities of proving and explaining, the data and the facts and the theories all follow.

Learning the proper use of the words "true" and "false" began with learning how to use "red" and "ball" correctly. We later invented the practice of "*proving*-true-or-false"—in order to distinguish *warranted* claims from mere decrees of authority or even lucky guesses. To "prove scientifically," we must test hypothetical connections through carefully designed experiments. This method of proof is what turns prediction into science.

To scientists, the question "Why?" is a request to engage in the practice of "*explaining*-why." Why does the sun rise in the sky? Because the earth rotates on its axis. Why is the light bulb hot? Because an electric current through the filament produces heat. Why are my muscles aching? Because I have a viral infection. Scientific explanations connect causes to effects in ever-finer chains of events that increase the success rate of predictions. The ideal is to describe a causal system in such detail that predictions routinely are highly successful. Scientists replace the push-and-move causation of everyday thinking with more subtle objects and properties, and with relationships based on statistics and probability.

Causal explanations are stories about why some predictions turn out to be true and others false. We explain why an object appears red to one observer but orange to another, why the billiard ball moves in space to one particular location on the table and not to another, why events take place at the time they do and not earlier or later. Predicting, proving, and explaining are interlocking concepts. We prove that an explanation is true by testing its predictions, and we explain why the truth of a prediction proves what we say it proves.

Swallowing the last drops of water,
I put the weightless plastic bottle
Back in my pocket.
I do not belong in the desert.
The fragile plants around me
Are alive only by ancient deals
Struck with their environment,
Deals that traded peculiar structures
For moisture—
Wispy filaments of grass,
Thorny tumors of cactus,
Gnarled and twisted woods.
These plants might not choose
To grow this way,
Given a choice.
But things are always
As they are
For a reason.
Creature of water,
I have inherited different deals—
And I do not belong
In the desert.

Part III: Everyday Thinking and Science

Everyday thinking and science have worked so well, we have evolved to thinking that every event has a causal explanation. We explain the sensation of color by the molecular structure of the object seen, the physical properties of light traveling from object to eye, the retina of the eye and cortex of the brain. We have explanations for perceptual error, optical illusion, and hallucination. If you can experience it, we can explain it—or at least explain it away. Seeing should be believing only if the belief is proven and explained. We have ceded to science the guardianship of the physical world "outside."

We believe that "proven" causes are real even when we cannot perceive them, as long as our explanations insist that they exist. I have never seen electrons, but believe that they exist, because they provide the best explanations for the data. Our physicists believe that subatomic particles, such as quarks and gluons, explain everything we now perceive, and we believe our physicists. For many of us, such is the dominance of scientific explanation over everyday thinking. Should we cede to scientists the guardianship of not only everything that is *perceived*, but also everything that is *real*? We are not sure whether we should. Thus far, we manage to have it both ways at once, the clash of science with everyday thinking notwithstanding.

Scientific measuring, predicting, and explaining are communal practices coordinated by scientific language. It is too soon to know the scope of their ultimate success or failure. With regard to certain kinds of events, they have so far enjoyed a remarkable run at the betting table. But how much should we wager on them next time?

PART IV

Communities of Meaning

HUMAN PRACTICES AND LANGUAGE develop together, each influencing and penetrating the other. Using the analogy of thought and language as a road system, with meaningful locutions being the analogs of interconnected streets and roadways, then what we call "concepts" are popular itineraries, much like typical routes to get across the city or common vacation packages. Concepts are package deals tying human practices to particular words, as well as practices to practices, words to words, and even concepts to concepts. Concepts are the architectural wonders of language and thought. When a concept becomes established as a practice or method, we say that the words involved have acquired a meaning.

Practices, concepts, and words develop and exist within human "communities of meaning." Scientific communities, for example, promote the production of statements considered true by inventing methods for measuring, predicting, and explaining. Thousands of other communities, large and small, pursue other goals, developing their own practices, concepts, and words. They might not talk of "accurate" or "true," but use instead words like "good" or "just," "beautiful" or "graceful" or "sacred."

Communities of meaning develop their own sub-systems of roads—the streets of residential developments, commercial

Part IV: Communities of Meaning

areas, and entire cities. These sub-systems co-exist with the systems of practices created by everyday thinking and by scientific communities.

10

Morality and Law

THE FUTURE MAY BE a void with indefinite possibilities, but human actions in the past and present can help some possibilities become actual, rather than others. Such is our common-sense experience, reflected in our language. Communities therefore invent practices and words that help channel their members' actions, give their members goals, and evaluate methods of achieving those goals. The question "What should I do?" is answered with community stories about heroes or saints, with practices and principles of morality, and with talk about "good" and "evil," "right" and "wrong," "rights" and "duties."

Life evolves community and community evolves governance. Every community with a collective interest in the future has some code of conduct for its members, no matter how limited. Laws are words drafted to express and implement that communal code of conduct. Laws document the already-decided communal practices toward possible events.

People in community maintain their practices and laws for various purposes. Survival requires food and water, clothing and shelter, medicine and knowledge and skills. In order to secure these things, communities develop the concepts of person and property, obligation and ownership, contract and compensation. We design such concepts to promote future survival and protect past achievements.

Part IV: Communities of Meaning

Different communities tell different stories about the justification for their laws. Some say that their laws are the decrees of divine or human rulers to their subjects. Others say that their laws derive from the will of the governed, through law-governed processes.

Whatever the origin story for a set of laws, natural events and human desires create new pressures to change them. To decide which actions are "justified," we develop the concepts of the rule of law—justice and fairness, due process and equal treatment. These concepts provide an alternative to "immoral" and "unjust" uses of force, as well as a "justification" for the existence of the community itself and for its particular codes of conduct.

Peacekeeping missions
And community policing,
Imprisonment,
Confiscation,
And entitlement—
All are coordinated domination
By the community.
Who gets to say
What we shall do to them?
Who gets to say
What you can do to me?
Someone always gets to say,
Even with anarchists.
The power of the people
Always means
A few people will have power—
To lock me in the prison,
To lock me in the army,
To lock me in the fear
Of their power.
At least with laws,
"Unlawful" has a meaning,
And we both know it.

Part IV: Communities of Meaning

In our thinking about what we ought to do, there are always tensions between the individual and the group, between the practical and the ideal, between our pursuit of private interests and our desire to participate in community.

As populations grow, we need to act privately and collectively to provide food and build shelter, bring water and remove waste, produce goods and distribute them—all while protecting the environment. As our problems grow, so does the problem of deciding which problems need solutions and which solutions are worth attempting. Fights over water become struggles over the laws governing water. Fights over wealth become struggles over tax laws and payment programs. Struggles over laws become contests over the laws governing law-making and enforcement. To the extent that we resolve disputes peacefully, we resolve them using words and concepts, within the practice of argument. Legal concepts that prove acceptable evolve as parts of the community language. Legal concepts and rules evolve from the linguistic battlegrounds of civilization.

Political communities are the most ruthless communities of law. They use their own laws to justify controlling all people and things found within their geographic boundaries. Standing armies of word warriors impose peace throughout the countryside. But as our concepts of morality merge with the concepts of law, both become instruments of power. Words like "just" and "fair" appear on the pennants of the powerful, as well as in the pleas of the powerless. Such words inevitably become the casualties of war.

11

Aesthetics and Art

THERE IS TYPICALLY A tension between the pragmatic and the beautiful. Everything is more or less useful and more or less beautiful. From how I place the food upon the plate to how I hold my hand or say my words, every action can be performed more or less beautifully. Art acts primarily to create the beautiful, but every human action can be performed "artistically."

While scientific communities extend everyday thinking by predicting and explaining, and communities of law extend common wisdom by refining the practices of justice and fairness, artistic communities show us the limits of language by creating the indescribably beautiful. Art is the emphatic assertion, over and over, that there is more in experience than language can name and thought can understand.

Artists refuse to consent to the fiction that thought and language capture all there is. They constantly blur the lines that language draws and the things that thought conceives. Artists exploit the tension with the practical to make us self-conscious about the limitations of language. By fusing perceptions with emotions, moods with thoughts, space with time, the inanimate with the animate, artists show us that the lines we draw are merely pragmatic lines.

Architecture re-creates space in the image of the human spirit. It enshrines mood and thought in a place—installing the beautiful in precisely the same location as the practical. Sculpture materializes mind, leaving sensation and emotion and thought standing by themselves in marble or bronze.

Music, dance, song, and drama re-enact time as human experience. They compress and expand the flow of time in tempo with the human spirit. By actively creating the eternal within finite performances, they proclaim the uniqueness of the universal.

Literature is the most audacious art. It uses language to demonstrate the limits of language. Poetry leads us by unaccustomed paths to places where we know we can no longer name or think. We can only be aware that words are no longer adequate.

Poetry pushes language
To the breaking point—
Welding words together
At the margins of their meaning,
Building extraordinary thoughts
Out of ordinary sounds.
Poetry challenges the universe
And the human spirit
To create
What it imagines,
To imagine
What it conceives,
To experience
What is beyond conception—
Soft sounds
Breathing life
Into unsuspecting stone.
Poets believe in us
More than we believe
In ourselves.

Part IV: Communities of Meaning

Artists are people in civilized rebellion. Against words and language, they fight with paint and marble and metal. Against predicting, they rejoice in the unexpected. Against the causal order, they propose the impossible. Against law and domination, they revel in anarchy and freedom. Against the practical, they espouse the impractical. If artists seem preoccupied with mood, emotion, and spirit, it is because thought and language are too often preoccupied with everyday thinking and science.

As with all human activities, artistic rebellions are usually more effective when carried out by communities. Even the most solitary artist works out of communities of meaning that are organized around techniques, forms, or media. Modes of expression become methods for expression only in community.

Everyday thinking develops words to talk about beauty and art, but artists ensure the failure of everyday thinking. Their works defy definition, resist conceptualization, and refuse to submit to analyses of meaning. Trying to say what "beauty" and "art" mean, or what it is that makes beautiful things beautiful, is a symptom of a disease brought on by language. To pursue beauty we must be willing to turn our backs on definition, classification, and language. We must be willing to leave the road system and travel cross-country.

12

Mysticism and Religion

WE ARE ALL MYSTICS, just as we are all artists and judges and scientists. The mystical side of us tries to transcend the limits of thought and language by resolving all the tensions found within our experience.

Mysticism accepts no division between thoughts and things, inside and outside, scientific explanation and poetry. From the mystical standpoint, every thing that exists belongs in every one of those categories. Every human experience fuses sensation and emotion, the practical and the beautiful, reaction and action and inaction. We simultaneously see beauty in things, create beauty in things, and are things of beauty.

Artists point beyond language by re-arranging the categories invented by thought. They disconnect whatever thought and everyday thinking connect, and connect whatever thought insists on separating. Emotion is carved in stone, imagination is depicted as reality, beauty is elevated above survival. Artists give their witness through rebellion against language.

Mystics give their witness through civil disobedience and dissenting acceptance. Mystics project their awareness beyond thought and language by re-uniting what everyday thinking and science analyze and classify. Mystics become aware of the boundaries of their fields of vision by staring straight ahead until all distinctions within the field disappear. In an effort to be all-inclusive, mystics take the side of the victim, the disfavored, the outcast. Mysticism appears to be passive because it absorbs within itself the aggressiveness of thought and language.

While art redesigns the furniture of the universe to show us that it can be done, mysticism embraces all the furniture at once—both its design and arrangement. Both artists and mystics, however, are perfectly aware that it is only furniture.

Religious communities give symbolic expression to the mystical experience. Religions are communities of meaning whose stories, rituals, symbols, and concepts affirm the lives of exemplary people who have embraced the mystical. Individuals in religious communities share the conviction that mysticism is possible, valuable, beautiful, and real. They extol what is beyond language by celebrating the limits of the human.

Mystics embrace all things
So they can gaze beyond them—
Through the window
Of space and time,
Through the window
Of thought and language,
In a direction
That thoughts and photons
Cannot go.
While caught in contemplation,
We are free of thoughts and fears,
Free of life and death,
Absolutely free
And unconnected.
When it is over,
There are no memories of it,
Or words to describe it—
For there never were
Any particular things
To describe.
We are never really sure
It ever happened.

Part IV: Communities of Meaning

It is not possible to think or talk meaningfully about "a reality beyond language," any more than it is possible to imagine the furthest place with no space beyond it or the final second with no time after it. Thinking about what is beyond thought, describing what is beyond language, is like that. A person who finds a way to travel to the edge of thought and language cannot see any *thing* beyond that horizon, cannot think or describe any *thing* beyond it. Words and thoughts and things are mirror reflections of each other within consciousness.

The mystic can say nothing at all about the mystical experience, but better understands what the activity of "saying" is and what it is not. The mystic knows that when words and thoughts stop flowing, it is only a flow of words and thoughts that has stopped.

There can be no memories of what it was like beyond thought and language. But after experiencing the mystical, we live in the universe differently than we did before.

The awakening from the mystical to the everyday activities of the religious community can be a lonely form of heartbreak. The mystic has to watch as members of religious communities use words and symbols not only to calm fears but also to create guilt, not only to provide havens but also to incite riots, not only to give hope but also to subjugate and enslave. No human use of language can be nobler than the person using it. For the mystic, who must embrace all people and all things as they are, this heartbreak is perhaps the best evidence that the mystical experience is real.

PART V

Beyond Language

WE CAN FIND IN every thing degrees of reality and fairness and beauty and harmony. These are universal dimensions of individual things. Transcendence, however, is never found among things or predicated of things, for it is the very possibility of there being any things at all. We cannot experience transcendence, because it makes experience possible. What is beyond language cannot be named or thought, because it is presupposed by language and thought.

We are tempted to say that "transcendent being exists beyond language"—but then "being" and "exists" and "beyond" could not have their usual meanings. Using the analogy of thought and language as a system of roads, and of thinking and talking as journeying within that system, then transcendence is what makes such road systems and journeying possible.

The experience of transcendence results from a certain kind of self-reflection while on a thought journey. Such a mode of journeying is mindful of the "fact" that it is a thought journey that I am making. The difficulty is in talking about the road system as though it itself were merely a location within the road system. I can only explore within the system, never outside of it, but in doing so I can become convinced that there *is* a system, that it is a *system*, and that *I* am traveling in it.

13

The Universe

"The universe," we say, is the totality of all real things. It is the totality of all things that could be named as subjects of true statements. It is the sum of everything we could know, which includes everything that anyone could ever know.

The universe includes not only physical objects in space and time, but space itself and time itself. Space has the potential for infinite width, as well as infinite density. Space may now be billions of light years across, but there is infinite room for it to grow. There may be such things as the smallest objects in space, but any space they occupy can be subdivided still.

Time has the potential for infinite duration, as well as infinite density. The potential of the future to replenish the present is infinite. The time from the beginning of the physical universe to the present we now think to be about thirteen billion years, but we might revise this estimate upwards. We can divide any single second into a billion parts, but need not stop dividing.

As potentially infinite as they are, space and time and the physical objects in them are only parts of the universe. The universe includes all true relationships among objects—all events and actual changes and causal actions. The universe also includes all real sensations and perceptions, all actual hallucinations and memories, all emotions and moods. It includes all thoughts, and therefore all predictions and explanations, laws and nations, symphonies and symphonic performances, and every character that Shakespeare ever imagined. It includes irrational numbers, quark theories, land-use plans for cities, and social classes based on income. Everything named by a true statement is real. The universe is the totality of whatever exists, has existed, or will exist, whether any one ever names them or not, thinks about them or not.

It is clear that I can neither imagine nor understand such a universe. It is clear that no one ever could. It is not that the universe is too extensive for me to imagine—as though the universe is only space. It is not that the universe is too long-lasting—as though the universe is only a matter of time. The trouble is not that the universe is infinite in these dimensions, but that it has an infinite number of possible dimensions, of which space and time are only two.

Thousands of millions of galaxies,
Each with
Hundreds of millions of stars,
All fleeing into space,
And into the future.
We are being left behind
To dream—
Of space travel,
Of time travel,
Of mind travel.
We long to be out there,
Looking around.
But in thought
And imagination
We are already out there—
We bring
The out-there
Here,
And conceive it
To be
Like us.

Part V: Beyond Language

You and I now exist at what we call a single moment within time—we are events within threads of causes stretching from the very beginning through the present to the end. The universe includes all we have discovered, plus everything that anyone could ever someday discover. Life in other star systems, time travel through warps in space and time, paranormal powers of the mind—these are possibilities we now believe might be real. Whether they *are* in fact real, you and I will probably never know. We can conceive only a small portion of reality, and must be wholly ignorant of everything beyond our current practices, concepts, and words.

The universe by definition "contains" every "thing" that is real. It is the name for the totality of everything that can be truly named. The universe therefore includes itself. It is the set of all sets, including the set that is the universe itself. Our concept of the universe spirals out of control trying to catch its own tail—it includes itself within itself, and includes *that* entity within itself, and so on *ad infinitum*, seemingly forever.

The *concept* of "the universe" is so strange, we should wonder why we have invented it at all. Perhaps only mystics and artists appreciate its usefulness, as a word pointing to the possibility of endless naming. Using the concept of "the universe" expresses our conviction that language and thought set the bounds of everything. Yet all meaningful use of language can invoke that conviction. To question whether there exists anything beyond thought and language makes no sense, yet somehow perfect sense.

14

God

I cannot understand why, if God exists, evil events occur. If I were God, I would intervene to keep buses of children from falling off cliffs; I would prevent cancers from growing in stomachs; I would prohibit drought, produce and distribute enough food, reform the thoughts of people who intend to hurt other people. Being impartial, I would intervene whenever danger threatens any of the billions of people on the planet. If a just and powerful God existed, there would be more miracles.

On the other hand, I literally cannot imagine what such a world would look like, for the causal regularities we now find in nature would necessarily disappear, drowned in a sea of inexplicable rescues. But any benevolent God would try to create such a world. We use the concept of God when we think that, although objects and events in space and time do not care about you and me, we care about them and about each other. Life is not fair, but it should be. Our concept of "God" expresses our estrangement from the "outside" world described by science.

Some communities select the words they value most and use them to describe God. God is a "powerful," "good," and "just" "person." God is "real." But such descriptions make God something within the universe—someone or something capable of causing miracles within space and time. People who have this concept of God often wonder whether such a God exists.

Part V: Beyond Language

Some communities assert that God is beyond naming, description, language, and imagination. Using this concept of "God" to describe God implies the truth of the statement's negation, and therefore implies a contradiction. "God is good" entails that God is *not* "good," as we mean "good." "God is alive," but necessarily also *not* "alive," in our normal sense of "alive." "God is real," but *not* "real"—not part of the universe. Contradiction is essential to this concept of God. Such communities profess to deliberately break the rules of grammar, as a way of insisting that God is beyond naming and language. God is not good, but "Goodness." God does not think, but is rather "Thought Itself." The goal is to nullify naming, disable description, derail language, and paralyze imagination—even just for a moment.

God

Hopeless as it seems,
People hunt for God
Everywhere—
In the sky and on mountaintops,
In desert quiet and ocean storms,
In conquest and love-making,
Community and ritual,
Thought and language.
People pray for signs and miracles,
Messages from outside
The universe—
As though we would not
Explain them away
As quickly as they occurred.
We can only see
What we can imagine,
And what we are
Is all that there can be.
Our thoughts
Are hands
Pressed against prison walls,
Unable to feel
The other side.

One use of the word "God" is the practice of refusing to name that which cannot be named. Even the assertion that God does not exist, if it is a true statement, entails its own negation, and therefore contradiction. That experience of contradiction is the experience of running headlong into the wall created by language and thought.

This *concept* of "God" is so strange, we should wonder why we have invented it at all. Using the word necessarily leads to endless contradictions—any thought about God attempts to name what cannot be named, which requires us to deny that God can be named, which is itself an assertion about God, *ad infinitum*, seemingly forever. Using the concept of "God" creates a short-circuit within thought itself.

But perhaps this is a fitting design for a concept of transcendence. The concept of God symbolizes the endless affirmation-and-negation that occurs when language and thought analyze-and-name, and then try to re-connect everything to everything. To use this concept is to remind ourselves of our imprisonment within language and thought. The practice of explicit contradiction about justice and goodness uses language to halt coherent thought. To question whether justice and goodness can occur beyond thought and language makes no sense, yet somehow perfect sense.

15

What I Am

WHAT WE ARE, OUR communities tell us, are objects at particular places and times. We can sense the colors that the world shows us, feel its warmth, and taste its saltiness. We can react in pain, feel sorrow, and be buoyed by optimism. We can name some of these sensations and feelings, and connect them into useful bundles, while overlooking and ignoring many more.

We also have knowledge of the objects beyond sensation and feeling. We can study the sun, not only feel its warmth. We can touch another's face, and remember the years that we have shared. We can hold hands, and can hope together for more years to come. Layer upon layer, our stories weave space and time together, the warp of physical objects supporting the threads of events.

Together we classify and count and measure, record the past, and predict the future—even search for causal chains to bend that future slightly to our wills. We explain why we can see and hear the objects that we do, and why we seem to see and hear things when we do not.

We can move easily from one community of meaning to another, participating fully in each without exclusion. Together we can search for scientific truth, mutually testing our assertions. We can pursue the good, evaluating our actions by our standards of justice and fairness. We can appreciate beauty in things, often creating it ourselves. We can comprehend all things in harmony together, resting in awe of their simplicity.

Part V: Beyond Language

The beginning of wisdom may be questioning and wonder, but the maturing of wisdom is the ability to find value, beauty, and belonging in the least significant grain of sand upon the beach.

We are "persons" who can know that we are parts of everything, and that there is something for us to be parts of. We can think or talk about every thing, yet know that we cannot think and talk about everything. We value infinite contradiction because it reminds us that we are capable of knowing and talking, yet limited by our thoughts and language. The use of language to demonstrate the limitations of language affirms the existence of a thoughtful self.

What I am
Is an endless procession
Of wonder-colored
Words and thoughts.
Creator of space,
In space.
Creator of time,
In time.
An epic story
Of joyful acts
And unconsoled weeping,
Hurtful acts
And penitent rejoicing.
A boundless circle
Bounding all,
Endless awe
Affirming and denying,
Point of origin
And final resting point.
I am spirit—
Object and subject,
Creator of self.

Part V: Beyond Language

What I am is a moment through which language flows. I am a tributary for the flow of language. Nearly everything I value would be impossible without language, including my consciousness. I am a creator and creation of language. As I explore the universe of things, try to peer outward from its boundaries, and stare inside its every point, I glimpse my own reflection in the mirror of language. What I see is what I am and think and say. Seeing my own reflection is not a matter of knowing where to look, or how to look, or when to look, but of realizing that I am looking.

The word "I" attempts to name the one who must exist un-named whenever naming occurs. "I" attempts to name the one who must exist un-thought whenever thinking occurs—even thoughts about me, for "I" am not "me." I am distinct from any things that can be thought or said about me. I am the possibility of thinking and talking about any thing in the universe.

The concept of "I" is so strange, we should wonder why we have invented it at all. I elude every attempt to capture myself in thought—any thought about me is a thought that I have, which generates another thought about me, which is a thought that I have, *ad infinitum*, seemingly forever. The concept of "I" includes an impossibility of being named that arises every time I name anything. It is a symbol of transcendent nothingness, an eternally invisible source of naming and thinking, a point of origin that takes up no space or time. The concept re-enacts the constant stream of sensing and feeling and naming and thinking that is my conscious reality. To question *what* I am besides my thoughts and language makes no sense, yet somehow perfect sense.

AFTERWORD

Who I Am

WHAT I AM IS a being capable of using language, but *who* I am is the story that I tell with language. I am this story and the telling of it. I am this flow of experiences and thoughts, this drama of these actions and emotions, this person in these relationships and communities. Every word that travels through my mind, or through my mouth, or through my pen, continues my conversation with the universe, with God, and with myself. Using language is ancient ritual coming to fulfillment in new creation. "Who am I?" is answered by the telling of the story that I am and choose to tell, using those rituals. Who I am is the stream of words and thoughts and deeds that I am becoming.

I am
These words and these thoughts,
But not only
These words and thoughts.
I am the inventor
Of words and thoughts
Themselves.
I am language and thought.
I am
These nine sunrises
Telling this story,
This warm wind
Reciting poetry
In desert morning air.
I am
This time and place
Where these words flow,
Obtaining my meaning
From somewhere
Beyond language.